TROPHIC CASCADE

Wesleyan Poetry

TROPHIC CASCADE

Wesleyan University Press | Middletown, Connecticut

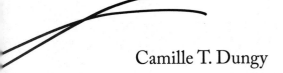

Camille T. Dungy

Wesleyan University Press
Middletown CT 06459
www.wesleyan.edu/wespress
© 2017 Camille T. Dungy
All rights reserved
Manufactured in the United States of America
First paperback edition 2018
ISBN for the paperback edition: 978-0-8195-7856-3
Designed by Mindy Basinger Hill
Typeset in Adobe Caslon Pro

The Library of Congress cataloged the hardcover edition as:
Names: Dungy, Camille T., 1972– author.
Title: Trophic cascade / Camille T. Dungy.
Description: Middletown, Connecticut : Wesleyan University Press, [2017] |
Series: Wesleyan poetry
Identifiers: LCCN 2016042846 (print) | LCCN 2016051445 (ebook) |
    ISBN 9780819577191 (cloth : alk. paper) | ISBN 9780819577207 (ebook)
Classification: LCC PS3604.U538 A6 2017 (print) | LCC PS3604.U538 (ebook) |
    DDC 811/.6—dc23
LC record available at https://lccn.loc.gov/2016042846

This project is supported in part by an award
from the National Endowment for the Arts.

ART WORKS.

**National
Endowment
for the Arts**
arts.gov

Contents

Natural History

The Rufous hummingbird builds her nest
of moss and spider webs and lichen.
I held one once—smaller than my palm,
but sturdy. I would have told Mrs. Jeffers,
from Court Street, if in those days of constant flights
between California and Virginia I'd wandered
into that Oakland museum. Any chance
I could, I'd leave my rented house in Lynchburg.
I hated the feeling of stuckness that old city's humidity
implied. You need to stop running away so much,
Mrs. Jeffers would say when my visits were over
and I leaned down to hug her. Why her words
come to me, the woman dead for the better part
of this new century, while I think of that
nest of web and lichen, I cannot rightly say.
She had once known my mother's parents.
The whole lot of them, even then, in their twenties,
must already have been as old as God. They were
black—the kind name for them in those days
would have been Negroes—and the daily elections
called for between their safety and their sanity
must have torn even the strongest of them down.
Mr. Jeffers had been a laborer. The sort, I regret,
I don't remember. He sat on their front porch
all day, near his oxygen tank, waving occasionally
to passing Buicks and Fords, praising the black
walnut that shaded their yard. She would leave
the porch sometimes to prepare their meals.
I still have her yeast roll recipe. The best
I've ever tried. Mostly, though, the same Virginian
breeze that encouraged Thomas Jefferson's
tomatoes passed warmly through their porch eaves
while we listened to the swing chains, and no one

talked or moved too much at all. Little had changed
in that house since 1952. I guess it's no surprise
they'd come to mind when I think of that cup
of spider webs and moss, made softer by the feathers
of some long-gone bird. She used to say, I like it
right here where I am. In my little house. Here,
with him. I thought her small-minded. In the winter,
I didn't visit very often. Their house was closed up
and overheated. Everything smelled of chemical
mothballs. She had plastic wrappers on the sofas
and chairs. Everyone must have once
held someone as old and small and precious as this.

4

Before the fetus proves viable,
a stroll creekside in the High Sierra

It seems every one is silvered, dead,
until we learn to see the living—
beaked males and females clutching
their hundred thousand roe—
working muscle, fin, and scale
against the great laws of the universe—
current, gravity, obsolescence, and the bears
preparing for their torpor, clawing
the water for weeks, this rich feed
better than any garbage bin—and these still
living red ones, who made it past all that,
nuzzling toward a break in the current,
everything about them moving, moving
yet hardly moving forward at all.

"still in a state of uncreation"

Little eradicator. Little leaser.
Little loam collector, connoisseur
of each vestigial part. Little bundle
of nerve. Waste leaker. Pump.
Little lead-in, lean-to, least known,
lucky landing. Bean, being, borne
by me. Little consequence.
Little ruckus causer. Unborn.
Little insatiable. Little irrevocable.
Little given. Little feared.
Little living. Little seen. Little
dangler. Little delight. Little
growing. Little life. Little you.

Ars Poetica: Mercator Projection

Windhoek to Walvis Bay

Pulp the plant and plant it new, that's what termites do. We learned that from books one devoured while the other was driving. From the conferences convened inside the car. We'd come down from the highlands. Come out of acacia trees and into acacia bushes. We taught ourselves to gauge the age of a termite mound by the age of the acacia beside it. We founded a college, which grew into a university, for we had space and time. I watched one colonial town fade from the rearview and then nothing until another white-washed town wavered in our windows, its petrol station in view a long while. I grew restless with little to do but stitch and re-stich my notions. We had assumed we would hop in the car and arrive there shortly. We hadn't adjusted our perspective yet. We wouldn't adjust our perspective for hundreds of years. I spied with my little eyes: several journeys of giraffe, a congress of baboons, a pride of ostrich (baby ostrich, mama ostrich, ostrich—gray and white and black of feather, gray and white and black of feather, gray and white and black of feather—of an uncertain age), kudu—brown and beige of pelt and antler, brown and beige of pelt and antler—and signs warning kudu jump into the road. Nearly indistinguishable from the bush, all this life lived on before us. We sighted oryx with black noses to draw heat off their brains, an implausibility of wildebeest, a band of mongoose, and several confusions of guinea fowl fowling the road. At first, we felt as close to God as Adam, and as headlong, naming every beast and bird and bush with plastic specificity. I didn't know an eland from a hartebeest, but the naming made them. We felt satisfied until we noticed how far we were past our star's highest hour. We had descended from bushes to succulents. Driven from succulents to little but lichen scattered close to the stony ground. *This reminds me of Lubbock, of the scratchy plains outside of Lubbock,* one of us noted, though the other was napping by then, head toppled like our top-heavy globe. *This reminds me of the moon.* It was not long before the gloaming of the first day in the furthest reaches of our dreams, when what we were seeing couldn't be compared to what we had seen. Rising in the distance could have been anything. Could have been fortresses. Could have been oceans. Could have been elephants. Could have been dunes. We were caught somewhere between the compact center of the earth and the earth's exaggerated edges. Trucks drove toward us with long fishing poles lodged in their front fenders. Trucks drove toward us looking like catfish on their way to a cove that was bound to disappoint. I thought I was close to understanding where we really were, but that ceased to be the point a long time ago. One of us passed a strip of dry, salty meat through our own lips. One of us passed a strip of dry, salty meat to the dog. We climbed out of the car inside a grayness and put up our tent in the wind. The sun set before we got the fire started. There were no stars to speak of, only fog and clouds and a long night sky, jackals packed and cackling in the distance, the road ahead of us still.

Ultrasound

I will wait for you as cicada wait
through winter, their August song
harbored in the last thunder clap
of the season. I will wait, as I wait
through any drought, for the lesson.

I will wait for you as the colloquy waits
on polyphony; wait for you as the bunting
waits on the berry. I will wait for you,
as I wait through all the hedgerows.
I will wait for the clearing.

I will wait as the tide pool waits. I will
wait as the upturned leaf before dawn.
The hangar for its zeppelin. The student
for her marks. I will wait. I will wait,
untying lace, for the double binding.

As I wait for the green grandeur of luna moth,
wings once apprehended then gone
out of sight, I will wait for you. I will
wait as your infant tongue will wait,
unacquainted, for the first taste of cherry.

Ars Poetica: Cove Song

One and two and three: in time,
    white birds hum out of the choir
of air, while we tend our dark skin
    with coconut oil, content to sing
a welcome to the high and low tides.

    The sky song is a blues the sea
comes into on repeated lines. Why, even
    the rocks sing, the reeds. This
is how we learn what game to lure
    into what traps, which scales
to seek, which to keep at bay. We've heard
    the mess those men have said. That
all we do is stand around and chatter.
    It drives them mad, our simple acts
repeated for the pure pleasure of sound.

    We've taught the flowers, high
and yellow, how to modulate
    their tone. They used to come off sharp
and off-beat, but now they blend
    right in. The men think themselves
industrious. Sword thrusting,
    sea sailing: the purposes of their purpose
driven lives. It makes them crazy
    to think we do nothing more than play
the lyre, sing all day. Like a group
    of grade school boys trounced in debate,
they plug their ears and turn away.

Only one climbed the lookout
to listen. Does he hear? Even
       the boulders' jaws are wide,
even the canoe's mouth joins our song.
       The cloud is singing softly. Listen now,
her voice will blend with wind, with rain.

Nullipara

I have learned love rests on the odd assortments of petals.

Pick buttercup, pick sweet pea:
You love me. You love me.

Pick snowdrop:
You love me not.

What then shall I make of the four valves in your heart?
The twin seedpods of your ovaries?

You love me not. You cannot love.

I dream of the digits, five on each
of the hands I am hoping to hold.

Your ten toes curl and uncurl through the sea
of my unseeing.

Ars Poetica: Field Trip

They hate this stuff, want them some chicken, she said, tossing bored yard dogs boneless breasts of chicken. We understood what she meant only when the crate had been opened and five de-beaked birds stopped flapping their fleshed and feathered carcasses around the yard, bodies assigned to one pile, heads to another. The dogs drooled, but by then the children's heads were mostly bowed or covered. Sharmaine pulled her little brother's body to her chest. Maybe she was crying, though with her I can never quite tell and Tyrone was sitting all of a sudden, crouching really, and biting his knee to hold back tears. You can't do that, we said, but of course it had already been done, and she couldn't see why not, she'd grown up here, and what was it we'd brought the kids to see? The sterile packages she'd send to market later? *In the old days birds fought back*, she said, assuming it was the speed of the dispatch that alarmed us. *I once gave up a goose what got away 71 times, ran round this damn yard near all afternoon before Old Bo got a grip on her and lost an eye for his trouble. These de-beaked things, they have no fight,* she said, her hands slick from tossing expired breasts to distract the dogs, a ruddy feather planted just above her lip. On her signal, Frankie and Will opened another crate and several necks were simply severed. Bo, one eye open, head square on his paws, kept the young ones in their corner. Those dogs, they licked each other's muzzles and their own.

Trophic Cascade

After the reintroduction of gray wolves
to Yellowstone and, as anticipated, their culling
of deer, trees grew beyond the deer stunt
of the mid century. In their up reach
songbirds nested, who scattered
seed for underbrush, and in that cover
warrened snowshoe hare. Weasel and water shrew
returned, also vole, and came soon hawk
and falcon, bald eagle, kestrel, and with them
hawk shadow, falcon shadow. Eagle shade
and kestrel shade haunted newly-berried
runnels where mule deer no longer rummaged, cautious
as they were, now, of being surprised by wolves. Berries
brought bear, while undergrowth and willows, growing
now right down to the river, brought beavers,
who dam. Muskrats came to the dams, and tadpoles.
Came, too, the night song of the fathers
of tadpoles. With water striders, the dark
gray American dipper bobbed in fresh pools
of the river, and fish stayed, and the bear, who
fished, also culled deer fawns and to their kill scraps
came vulture and coyote, long gone in the region
until now, and their scat scattered seed, and more
trees, brush, and berries grew up along the river
that had run straight and so flooded but thus dammed,
compelled to meander, is less prone to overrun. Don't
you tell me this is not the same as my story. All this
life born from one hungry animal, this whole,
new landscape, the course of the river changed,
I know this. I reintroduced myself to myself, this time
a mother. After which, nothing was ever the same.

After Birth

The new mothers sleep, always, in their clothes
since all their doors have been opened,

since they learned every room is a part of every other room.

The new mothers are just like the old mothers.

Common as suburban deer, the new mothers see human faces,
human faces, human faces, all these windows,
        every garden trampled, every feeder
emptied to spite hunger not as lovely as a birds',

        and winter coming on.

About time, the new mothers are cooperative.

They measure months by the length of an arm,
the proportion of leg muscle to belly fat.

        They will wait several weeks for a minute.

            The trees dropped their fruit and all of us
            were drawn to it. Was a time, before,
            when this field was wide and welcoming.

Every door has been opened. Empty windows,
empty windows, empty windows, now, their wombs.

        The new mothers live in the open, pacing the hours.

About dreams, they are like animals,
the new mothers.

Mouths to feed and flanks to warm.

Everything cleared out
and winter coming on.

Frequently Asked Questions: #1

Is she talking yet?

She curses like a scholar.

She says "MMMMMMM fffffffffffff thhhhthththth"
   which roughly translates to, "May your fate be like that of Thebes."

      Her look is menacing.

I do her bidding and she retracts her curse
      saying, "Ahhhh ahhhh gah wa wa."

      I take this to mean, "I am the wise one.
I am the one who will steer you. Well done. Well done."

Frequently Asked Questions: #2

Is it true that once you're a parent it's hard to maintain
a social life of your own?

At the nursery, I met Elder Happy, father of 13, teacher, wandering scribe.

I'd read his books for years, couldn't believe my luck
        meeting Elder Happy in the flesh.

The Elder was reliably happy. He told me he was happy
        to meet another new mother.
He was happy to help with my sleep deprivation. He was happy
        to see the fullness I still carried through my thighs.

The milk dream of my breasts made him happy.
                My half alert eyes.

Ars Poetica after William Carlos Williams

If when my hubby is sleeping
and the baby and Vanessa
are sleeping
and the sun is a yellow-gray Frisbee
in nets of fog
caught in burled trees—
if I in my kitchen
wrote poems unceasingly
at my table
twirling my hair round my finger
and whispering softly to my old self:
"I am awake now, awake.
I have always been awake,
it is just so!"
If I admire my fingers, their grip,
the muscle in my arm, breasts
full with uncried for milk—

Who is to say I am not
the fortunate creator of my household?

Frequently Asked Questions: #3

Does she sleep through the night?

I hate to wake you so early,

but I had to tell you

this dream.

There were only seven trees left in the world

and the largest grew in your backyard.

Ars Poetica Apocalyptica

the boy walks me to the near edge of the purple horizon

      past the last of the strip malls
past the dancing rebels   the food trucks   the penny-saver girl

keys bell his belt loops and pockets
                keys jangle his necklace   castanets
    in his small calloused hands

                  the boy walks with me
toward bubble-roofed aluminum trailers and a horizon the color of plums

    keys sprout from the dirt at our feet
the way it used to be with clover

      I don't understand all the keys   so I ask

the boy squats to collect what the dirt has offered

      who can know what they will open?
      the keys have flimsy rings and illegible labels
    they all look the same   though some of them are different

      This looks like the key to my mother's car.
A church key! The office?

the boy collects keys from the shady earth
                the way we used to collect chanterelles

This might be the key to my house.

at the near edge of the belligerent horizon the boy turns a key over twice
    before he slips it in his pocket

then he tosses a ring in the air the way we once tossed tangerines

Last Kiss

Mom called tonight. Just to hear
my voice. She'd spent a long day
ushering at a funeral. A thousand
people: every seat in the sanctuary,
chairs in the narthex, the fellowship
hall. People lined up since seven this
morning. A 17-year-old—volleyball star,
newspaper editor—riding home from youth
group. Her organs, eyes, ligaments, & skin were
rushed elsewhere in lifecopters. One mother—her daughter
completed suicide two years before—told the other volunteers
she came to acknowledge how they helped her. *I know I never
thanked you. Every time I went to write a card*, she said,
I couldn't. My friend Sebastian was in a wreck last
week. His heart is bruised. What happens when
a heart is bruised? Caterpillars live
in the passion flower bush over
my girl's daycare. When
I kissed her goodbye
this morning, nine
butterflies circled
my head.

Glacial Erratics

There are people who, when they go, shift
the meaning of words we use each day.

        Down goes Frazier,
we used to joke, when sleep knocked our daughter out.

    Now Frazier's dead,
        and Megan's mom is dying of the same cancer.

On the phone last night, Megan was a baby.
            So many new words
she needed to say, but no better way to speak than by crying.

    A wrack of grief we used to say,
          meaning shipwreck,
   souls sunk, lost
      fortune, meaning ruin.

Though wrack can also mean seaweed, vegetation,
    can mean what grows up from what has fallen.

A whale fall can support life for over seven decades.
    The grotesque
and beautiful blooming

    off a mortal behemoth.
        Bone-rooted worms
waving like marsh grasses.
   Hagfish, all saw-mouth and mucous.
        Brittle stars.

When she got her words again, Megan said the worst of it
was that her mother was still driving her crazy.

I want to kill her,
said Megan. *Does she always have to be so controlling?*

The morning she chose to join us, my daughter pushed against me.
My whole body, becoming a mother,
squeezed, trying to help push her along.
And what could she do
but push against me again?

Down goes Frazier, we joked
because she fought so hard to be alive she hated ever to leave us.

Once, my whole body, becoming a mourner, had to push my girl out,
to let her go. Like this
we'll be pushing each other, until one of us is finally done.

Conspiracy

to breathe together

Last week, a woman smiled at my daughter and I wondered
if she might have been the sort of girl my mother says spat on my aunt
when they were children in Virginia all those acts and laws ago.

Half the time I can't tell my experiences apart from the ghosts'.

A shirt my mother gave me settles into my chest.

I should say *onto my chest*, but I am self conscious—
the way the men watch me while I move toward them
makes my heart trip and slide and threaten to bruise
so that, inside my chest, I feel the pressure of her body,
her mother's breasts, her mother's mother's big, loving bounty.

I wear my daughter the way women other places are taught
to wear their young. Sometimes, when people smile,
I wonder if they think I am being quaintly primitive.

The cloth I wrap her in is brightly patterned, African,
and the baby's hair manes her alert head in such a way
she has often been compared to an animal.

There is a stroller in the garage, but I don't want to be taken
as my own child's nanny. (Half the time I know my fears are mine alone.)

At my shower, a Cameroonian woman helped me practice
putting a toy baby on my back. I stood in the middle of a circle
of women, stooped over and fumbling with the cloth. Curious George
was the only doll on hand, so the white women looked away
afraid I would hurt my baby while the black women looked away
and thought about not thinking about monkeys.

There is so much time in the world. How many ways can it be divided?

I walk every day with my daughter and wonder
what is happening in other people's minds. Half the time
I am filled with terror. Half the time I am full of myself.

The baby is sleeping on my back again. When I stand still,
I can feel her breathing. But when I start to move, I lose her
in the rhythms of my tread.

Frequently Asked Questions: #4

Does she have teeth yet? Does she bite you?

Months into our confinement I grew
a new set of ears, a heart, and a mouth I lent her
because she was so quiet I was almost alone.

She has taken my mouth and put her own tongue inside.
She has taken my heart and also my eyes.

She has taken my breasts
and put her own pleasure before them.

She bites beans and fields of solemn sweet potatoes root
for their own harvest.

She bites into a pear and every pearl
in the world releases its oyster.

She bites what flesh is offered and always finds more.

She has teeth, yes. She bites me
and the world gives up
its treasure.

All my dreams rising for her.
All those pearls.

Frequently Asked Questions: #5

Do you have big plans for her first birthday?

Tomorrow this will all be over. She will take a step
    and the tide that fills the tide pools will come in.

The last crop of almonds in the world must begin as nothing
    but a thousand thousand miniscule blossoms.

I have loved every cell of her body from the time I could count them
    until now.

Why hurry her progress when each day is as gorgeous as the last?

She will take a step and the beekeeper will plant his hives in the orchard,
    walk away.

Ars Poetica: After the Dam

the floodplains bloom   the horsetail dies   the wheat
with its combined eyes eyeing a fat future nods and nods never fearing

the peasants plant potatoes plant turnips radish and carrot

even the mice leave the hovels and make camp in the fields

when an inland bird calls from the roof thatch the boatwright turns
from bowsprits and trains his son to cobble

only that bright-chested bird knows the end of this song

but she is winging over water and must not waste her breath to sing

Mother daughter hour

Callie is reading the book about language,
and I am reading the book about death.

Ball, she says, pointing to an orange.
        I shake my head.

        I read, *Death is the mother of beauty*.
She says, *pretty ball*.

I am going to have to put down my book so I can teach her better,
        but first I read her one last sentence
        because I am struck by all its vowel sounds.

        That, finally, is all it means
    to be alive: to be able to die.

        She is listening
and she is not listening.

The afternoon light is brighter here on the couch than any other place
        in the room.

With her little thumb and baby fingers, my daughter turns
        her board book's pages.
                Red, she says,
        pointing to an apple.

Red, I say, and we sit together a while longer. Read some more.

Notes on what is always with us

This week I threw a birthday party for my mother, and grief came along
for the cake.

Ten mothers at my mother's birthday dinner,
three of them bereaved of a child.

The dead celebrated right there with the living.

We asked grief to be quiet, but she smiled, smacked her lips,
and tore into her steak.

33

On land, adult penguins have no natural predators.

The big bad wolf is not, in Antarctica, a problem.
No lions, no tigers, no bears.

Penguin eggs and penguin chicks are always at the mercy
of skua and disaster, but even from the leopard seal and orca
the land hauled adult penguin is safe.

I am trying to write about penguins, about predatorless terrains.
I am trying to write about joy and a kind of cold beauty,
but grief won't stay away.

Grief will ride in on the smallest of bodies,
a tick on a cormorant's wing.

If the winter isn't cold enough to kill it, that tick will embed itself
in a penguin's neck, the back of her head, anywhere
the penguin can not reach,
and because she has no way to tell anyone
and because, even if she could convey her agony,

there would be no way for her fellow birds to help,
she will itch for awhile, swell for awhile,
then abandon her nest for the water's relief.

She will run and slide and dive into danger.

Her eggs will die and her chicks will die
and she may die as well.

I am trying to write about predatorless terrains,
but grief will ride in on the smallest of bodies,
a tick on a cormorant's wing.

I try to write everything down, because I know it would be easier
to forget and I want to
avoid the comforts of suppression.

Scouring journals for my notes about seabird ticks and their toll
on Antarctic penguin populations, I find a different set of notes.
I'd written, *The only time I really talked to you was in your Trenton kitchen.*
What I meant was that was the only time I ever saw you genuinely smile.

The baby needed food, and you,
just back from pushing his stroller on a long walk
during which you and he both watched the morning sun shine
on the faded splendor of those Trenton streets,
were boiling a hot dog for your only son, and smiling.

There are things I do not want to say, I said in my journal.
Except the not saying won't return anything you love.

The boy is dead. The boy's mother is dead.

I was trying to write about beauty, but grief won't stay away.

I was trying to write about babies and birthdays and birds.
I was trying to write about joy.

There are these moments of permission

Between raindrops,

space, certainly,

but we call it *all* rain.

I hang in the undrenched intervals,

while Callie is sleeping,

my old self necessary

and imperceptible as air.

Because it looked hotter that way

we let our hair down. It wasn't so much that we
worried about what people thought or about keeping it real
but that we knew this was our moment. We knew we'd blow our cool

sooner or later. Probably sooner. Probably even before we
got too far out of Westmont High and had kids of our own who left
home wearing clothes we didn't think belonged in school.

Like Mrs. C., whose nearly unrecognizably pretty senior photo we
passed every day on the way to Gym, we'd get old. Or like Mr. Lurk
who told us all the time how it's never too late

to throw a Hail Mary like he did his junior year and how we
could win everything for the team and hear the band strike
up a tune so the cheer squad could sing our name, too. Straight

out of a Hallmark movie, Mr. Lurk's hero turned teacher story. We
had heard it a million times. Sometimes he'd ask us to sing
with him, T-O-N-Y-L-U-R-K Tony Tony Lurk Lurk Lurk! Sin

ironia, con sentimiento, por favor, and then we
would get back to our Spanish lessons, opening our thin
textbooks, until the bell rang and we went on to the cotton gin

in History. Really, this had nothing to do with being cool. We
only wanted to have a moment to ourselves, a moment before Jazz
Band and after Gym when we could look in the mirror and like it. June

and Tiffany and Janet all told me I looked pretty. We
took turns saying nice things, though we might just as likely say, Die
and go to hell. Beauty or hell. No difference. The bell would ring soon.

Poor Translation

(trans/la/tion (n): to shift a word or phrase from one language to another giving it equivalent meaning; to change from one state, place, or form to another; the linear movement of a body in which every point of the body follows a straight path and does not rotate.)

We knocked her down. She was lovely waisted
as she fell,
and she spun

down like a maple pod,
two arms stretched from the hard center.

This is what we wanted

because we were afraid. Ding dong, we sang.

Ding dong.

But she was not yet
dead, and so we sang no further.

"Why," the young ones asked, "why." And, "Why!"
and, "Why?" We didn't immediately

answer. For a moment, anyway, we'd forgotten ourselves
watching, as we had so long, her downward spiral,

but one of us finally spoke, and the rest corroborated
his story. The fact,
we'll admit, is we were disturbed
by the pleasure she took from our men.

At the market, we watched her, she had no shame.
Snatched Stan Samson's eye right along
—and he was not alone, we knew—
with the optic nerve and, still smiling, of course—imagine

the pleasure in that pretty package:
brown eye, in her purse now, the nerve
—sauntered on, plucky as you will.

She drank, we supposed, sangria*, by the bucket,

and all the eyes were on her—

some in her pocket, some in her purse,
some wrapped in a hanky and stuffed down her shirt—

all the eyes were on her when she cocked
her head and wet her lips
and drank. (Note: We say it's *bleeding*.) Awful

to think she enjoyed it so much,

so don't ask why, we told the young ones.
They are watching now and asking
no longer why. They know now

what it is all about. "Oh!" They say. "My goodness,
look! Look at that witch," enjoying

now, just perfect, her fall.

From the First, the Body Was Dirt

for A.S.

Whose hands touched, first, the head
of the penis, the shaft?

And was it soft
        or shale? More rock
than clay.

And who pinched first
into their place the small cups
at the base of the ass?

        Who was it
got down there, on whose knees,
and blew—
        and was that passion
or panic, the machine that drove
those exhalations?
        —and how
could we rate the power of that
breath—breeze or gale or a whisper
like the song the small boy sings
to the beetle,
        whose small legs moved in tune
like his legs, the legs on that first body, must have
moved, if they did move, when
        the dust settled.

In my mind everything's become enormous.

But was it ever small like that, the first body?

Did it ever sit close to the ants and their piles
of dirt from which that body had come?

You were a small boy once, I suppose.

You were dirty from the start.

You showed me how to use a cock ring,
and why.
         How, without ever paying
for a room, to spend two weeks in any city.
How two men could fuck
and continue to face each other
directly
       —took my body and showed me,
my back on a table, my knees by my head.
Stretched me
         into seeing you were more than a dog.

You must be dead by now, though I don't know
whose hands prepared you.

      Whose fingers
fingered, for the final time,
all that dark and kinky hair?

If the first body was made of dirt,
in order to plumb the hollow
of that first throat, whose thumb
first lodged inside the hinge
of that first mouth to force it open?

To make the tongue, so it could work,
who shoved inside that mouth
the shit of a hundred thousand worms?

Still life

Still life with Ensure, vials of fentanyl, oxycodone, water.
Still life with crackers maybe, hopefully, he will keep down.
Still life with tossed sheets and yogurt cup. Still life
with *Sports Illustrated* piles in the bathroom, guest room,
on the living room floor, on the dining room table, in recycle bins waiting
near the door. Still life with the younger brother assessing
how to dispose the hoardings of the one man left who shares his face.
Still life with hanging tension and sadness, failed ambition,
medicated dreams. Still life with phlegm and corruption.
With waste, with fanned get well cards, appointment reminders,
hospital garage parking receipts. Still life with the mantel clock,
one birthday's present, still ticking and ticking and ticking away.

Characteristics of Life

A fifth of animals without backbones could be at risk
of extinction, say scientists.
—BBC Nature News

Ask me if I speak for the snail and I will tell you
I speak for the snail.
                    I speak of underneathedness
and the welcome of mosses,
                                        of life that springs up,
little lives that pull back and wait for a moment.

I speak for the damselfly, water skeet, mollusk,
the caterpillar, the beetle, the spider, the ant.
                                        I speak
from the time before spinelessness was frowned upon.

Ask me if I speak for the moon jelly. I will tell you
            one thing today and another tomorrow
        and I will be as consistent as anything alive
on this earth.

            I move as the currents move, with the breezes.
What part of your nature drives you? You, in your cubicle
ought to understand me. I filter and filter and filter all day.

Ask me if I speak for the nautilus and I will be silent
as the nautilus shell on a shelf. I can be beautiful
and useless if that's all you know to ask of me.

Ask me what I know of longing and I will speak of distances
        between meadows of night-blooming flowers.
                                        I will speak
            the impossible hope of the firefly.

44

You with the candle
burning and only one chair at your table must understand
such wordless desire.

To say it is mindless is missing the point.

Frequently Asked Questions: #6

Now that you have a child, has your writing practice changed?

Digging rock from hardscaped beds, I think,
is a bit like not writing poetry—like thinking
about writing poetry but digging rock from my backyard
instead. If you've never pulled rock, with your own
gloved hands, or a trowel, with a flat-headed shovel,
on your knees, or squatting, or half bending so
your back will hurt by nightfall, never learned how
best to corral the rugged little stones so you might
scoop them and haul them to a container that will bear them
away, turn them into some other fool's problem, or if you have
and your fingers remember like mine remember a day's work
that wore holes into sweet, pink, flowered, garden gloves—
though when I called it quits after laboring more hours
than I labored with my daughter, it seemed
I'd hardly cleared any rock at all—you might wonder
why, when my shovel came down on a pyramid
of knob-sized gray and white and speckled stones
near the struggling young juniper and opened
a nest of lice-small cream eggs and writhing red and black
bodies I checked first that these were not termites—
my mercy limited by my love for the wood and mortar
I call home—then replaced the river stones
on the teeming anthill and turned to clear rock
from some other section of my hardscaped bed.

Bîtan

probable root of bitter: biting, cutting, sharp

Once, she was a fierce dark girl whose tongue skipped—
top of mouth, teeth, teeth,

        top of mouth,

            teeth—

like double dutch was a word that meant her thoughts
cutting circles through the daybore.

               No chance
she'd be the one to trip and break rhythm.

Back then she could sit all day on her porch
memorizing the trees.

          She could be still.

The birds winged through leaves like they didn't know
anyone could hurt them.

            Once, she believed
steam curling off asphalt when summer rains stopped
      was a prophecy.

            She believed this
looked the way she would feel after touching
a man:
      her body clean
         and black
              and right:
something beautiful and painless rising up.

We passed the baby over the bed, and later we passed tissue,
     and her Bible with its onion skin pages, its highlighted lessons
and dog-eared parables she kept handy with bookmarks
     whose tassels hung and swayed as her hair
might have done when she was very sweet and very young,
     and when we had finished what reading we would read,
we stopped a little while to register the pleasant song
     the woman on the stereo was singing, and then the baby
cried for milk, and so we passed her back across the bed,
     which is when someone asked if there was any more water
and we passed the water over her lips with the swab the nurses gave us
     just for this, a square pink bubblegum lollipop looking deal
like the treats she used to give us when we were very sweet
     and very young, and someone came with roses,
and though we smelled the flowers because we hoped for something better
     than the smell that lingered all around us, hothouse flowers look alive
long after their lively smells have faded, so when someone came in
     with cards, we passed the cards and flowers over the bed and
stood them up with the other cards and flowers on the little stand of white
     plastic and chrome that passed for a bedside table in that place, and
when a friend came in who hadn't met the baby, we passed the baby
     over the bed and the friend said, *she's so sweet,* and when a cousin
came who knew things few of us knew, we listened to stories
     from when both of them were very young, and when someone cried
we passed the tissue over the bed, and when someone said, *she's so small*
     now, we remembered the pink square bubblegum lollipop swab,
and when the nurse said, *you can tell by how she breathes,*
     someone got the Bible from the little chrome and plastic stand,
and when someone said, *it's okay to leave,* we didn't want to
     do a thing, and though several days later someone told me

people somewhere in West Africa pass a baby over the bed
of a dying person to say there will always be new bodies
to celebrate and mourn, that night we only knew the baby needed a change
and someone had to take her, and so we passed the baby
over the bed and decided who would stay to watch her go.

Frequently Asked Questions: #7

Is it difficult to get away from it all once you've had a child?

I am swaying in the galley—working
       to appease this infant who is not

fussing but will be fussing if I don't move—
       when a black steward enters the cramped space

       at the back of the plane. He stands by the food carts
prepping his service. Then he is holding his throat

the way we hold our throats when we think we are going to die.
I'm sorry. I'm so sorry. He is crying. *My God. What they did to us.*

I am swaying lest my brown baby girl make a nuisance
       of herself, and the steward is crying honest man tears.

       *Seeing you holding your daughter like that—for the first time,
I understand what they did to us. All those women sold away*

       from their babies, he whispers. I am at a loss now.
Perhaps I could fabricate an image to represent this

       agony, but the steward has walked into the galley
of history. There is nothing figurative about us.

Brevity

As in four girls; Sunday
dresses: bone, ash, bone, ash, bone, ash, bone.

Addie Mae Collins — Cynthia Wesley — Carole Robertson — Denise McNair

Frequently Asked Questions: #8

Are you going to have another child?

No.

soldier's girl

While he was gone, Mrs. Jessup wanted someone around
who knew her son. So Mary went. Mostly to see
his trophy case. Mostly to trail the tension of her skin
along the etched brass that witnessed his victories.
Her palm cry quieted there, touching those lost spaces
inside his name. Mrs. Jessup thought he'd joined up
for freedom. Mrs. Jessup didn't know her son.
She thought he'd come home directly. But he didn't
go straight home the day he crossed the line
with nothing but his name. Instead, he'd thrown gravel
at Mary's window, and when she came running
to the yard, he told her why he'd enlisted. The recruiter promised
nothing more than a rifle, a backpack, and a hard time.
He told her no one had ever been straight with him before.
Then he kissed her. Kissed her like a man would kiss a woman
after their children were asleep. Kissed her as if, just that night,
his father's battle lost, they'd both held his body while he died.

What I know I cannot say

We sailed to Angel Island, and for several hours
I did not think of you. When I couldn't stop myself, finally,
from thinking of you, it was not really you but the trees,
not really the trees but their strange pods, blooming
for a while longer, a bloom more like the fringed fan
at the tip of a peacock's tail than anything I'd call a flower,
and so I was thinking about flowers and what we value
in a flower more than I was thinking of the island or its trees,
and much more than I was thinking of you. Recursive language
ties us together, linguists say. I am heading down this road.
I am heading down this road despite the caution signs
and the narrow shoulders. I am heading down the curvy road
despite the caution signs and the narrow shoulders
because someone I fell in love with once lived around here. Right there,
that is an example of recursive language. Every language,
nearly every language, in the world demands recursion.
Few things bring us together more than our need to spell out
our intentions, which helps explain the early-20th century
Chinese prisoners who scratched poems into walls on Angel Island,
and why a Polish detainee wrote his mother's name in 1922. I was here,
they wanted to tell us, and by here they meant the island
and they also meant the world. And by the island, they meant
the world they knew, and they also meant the world they left
and the world they wanted to believe could be theirs, the world they knew
required passwords. Think of Angel Island Immigration Station as purgatory,
the guide explained. He told tales of paper fathers, picture brides,
the fabrications of familiarity so many lives depended on. Inquiries
demanded consistency despite the complications of interpretation.
In English one would ask: How many windows were in your house
in the village? How many ducks did you keep? What is the shape
of the birthmark on your father's left cheek? In Japanese, Cantonese,
Danish, Punjabi, the other answered. Then it all had to come back
to English. The ocean is wide and treacherous between one

home and the other. There can be no turning back, no correction
once what is said is said. Who can blame the Chinese detainees
who carved poems deep into the wood on Angel Island's walls.
Who can blame the Salvadoran who etched his village's name.
Few things tie us together more than our need to dig up the right words
to justify ourselves. Travelers and students, we sailed into the bay,
disembarked on Angel Island. I didn't think about you.
Which is to say, the blue gum eucalyptus is considered a threat,
though we brought it across oceans to help us. Desired first for its timber,
because it grows quickly and was expected to provide a practical fortune,
and when it did not, enlisted as a windbreak, desired still
because it is fast growing and practical, the blue gum has colonized
the California coastal forests, squeezing out native plants, dominating
the landscape, and increasing the danger of fire. I should hate
the blue gum eucalyptus, but from the well of their longing,
by which I mean to say from their pods, you know what I mean
I hope, their original homes, from the well of their longing
blooms explode like fireworks. I love them for this. Do you hear me?
I absolve you. You are far too beautiful and singular to blame.

Assignment #3: Write About Your Favorite Book

I only know Dolly's mother loved her and Dolly knew this
    because of the many-colored coat her mother made—
    sewn of flowers snipped from flour sacks, bright rags
    Dolly grew to love—I know this much
because every year, as trees put on red and gold tops,
    one girl would decide her favorite book was Dolly Parton's,
and during peer evaluation, pulling her diamond cross
    against its thin thin chain, this girl would finish reading her draft
    and sigh a sigh that signaled to the class the time to talk had come
so, jodhpurs still muddy, a girl who came straight from the stables,
and a girl who cried when I criticized her papers' generalities
    ("childhood is a time of protected innocence,"
    "children get to play outside all summer,"
    "all girls have a favorite doll"),
and, this seemed to happen each October, a girl whose mother had gazed
    from the same window M, W, F at 11, too,
    having taken freshman comp in that same room,
and the one who hated to be stereotyped and started the club
    that got girls talking about new ways to demonstrate love,
and the one who, during orientation, must have bought her favorite t-shirt
    in every color, the college logo sealed over her heart and, writ large,
    the unofficial motto, "not a girls' school with no men,
    but a women's college with no boys,"
and the girl who got engaged at her high school graduation party,
    the girl who rarely spoke, who covered her mouth when she smiled,
and the girl from the Southside Virginia no-stop-light town
    who always reminded us her town had no stop light,
and even the girl who was never shy about saying she didn't know
    what the other girls were talking about,
    she'd grown up someplace completely different,
said, it's about having pride in who you are and where you come from
    and the professor wants to know if she stuck to her thesis
    and she stuck to her thesis and I wish I could
    sew I'd make myself a coat like that and I just love this book

and does she need to bring up that Bible story
and the Bible story is a bit confusing, I don't think she cited her sources
     she left out quotation marks I think she means Dolly
     loves the coat but when she writes I loved the coat
     it sounds like her and I like that I think that's okay
and I love this book and I think this is a great paper
     yeah I really like this paper
and I really love how she gets us to care about her
and I feel she has everything she needs
and I feel we know everything we need to know.

Frequently Asked Questions: #9

Don't you think you should have another child?

This girl I have is hardtack and dried lime
    and reminds me, every groggy morning,
what a miracle it must have been
    when outfitters learned to stock ship holds
with that one long lasting fruit. How the sailors' tongues,
    landing on its bitter brilliance, must have cursed
the curse of joy, as I did that morning the burst
    of water brought my sweet girl into our lives.

But, already, she hates me sometimes.
    Like I have sometimes hated my mother and she
must have sometimes hated her own.

After weeks at sea, the limes would desiccate and the meal
    fill with worms. They would have eaten
anyway, the sailors, but taken no pleasure from anything.
    Or taken no pleasure from anything but
the fact of their sustained lives. Which is to say it is all
    I can do, most days, not to swallow
her up and curse her maker, I swear. Like I have not
    sworn since the morning she was born.

Against Nostalgia

I suppose you have food there, too, but here it is summer
      and we have asparagus, avocado, and stone fruit.
I am so happy.

The yard trees of my youth yield more fruit than we can handle.

I was going to bake chicken with cherries and apricot,
      but already it is too hot. I can't turn on the oven.

      Sometimes I bite straight into plums.
Other times I slice them to serve on a platter.

      Sometimes I want to move away
so I must remember everything I used to love: stone fruit and asparagus,
draughts of eucalyptus carried through the window on the wind.

Where bushes periodically burn,
children fear other children: girls

whose scornings are flint on dry rock
which—don't we know—is all the heart afforded
a certain type: untended, magnifying boys.

oh fickle lens! oh smoke and smoldering beetle!
oh thwarted desire in foothills of brush
and now flame.

Frequently Asked Questions: #10

Do you see current events differently because you were
raised by a black father
and are married to a black man?

I am surprised they haven't left already—
things have gotten downright frosty, nearly unbearable.
A mob of them is apparently mouthing off outside

when I put down my newspaper and we all gather
to stand beside my daughter in the bay
of kitchen windows. Quiscalus quiscula:

This name sounds like a spell which, after its casting,
will make things crumble into a complement
of unanswerable questions. Though, if you need me

to tell you God's honest truth, I know nothing
but their common name the morning we watch them attack
our feeder. I complain about the mess they leave. Hulls

I'll have to sweep up or ignore. My father—
who I am thankful is still alive—says *We could use*
a different kind of seed. A simple solution. We want that

brown bird with the shock of red: the northern flicker.
We want western bluebirds, more of the skittish
finches. But mostly we get grackle grackle grackle

all day long. They scoff all we offer
and—being too close and too many—scare
other birds away. Still, can it be justifiable

to revile these harbingers? My husband says, *Look
at all those crackles.* I almost laugh at him,
but the winter air does look hurtful loud

around the black flock. Like static is loud when it sticks
sheets to sheets so they crackle when pulled
one from another. And sting. My father—who is older now

than his older brothers will ever be—promises
he will solve the problem of the grackles
and leaves the window to search for his keys.

The dawn sky—blue breaking into blackness—
is what I see feathering their bodies. The fence
is gray. The feeder is gray, the aspen bark. Gray

hulls litter the ground. But the grackles,
their passerine claws—three facing forward, one turned
back—around the roost bar of the feeder, are

so bright within their blackness, I pray they will stay.

How Great the Gardens When They Thrive

While wrens, one by one, resuscitate their small portion
of the light, yellow buses progress, leave their lots.

Goodbye scarlet fever. Help for influenza.
Penicillin, inoculation: The end of women,
with their children, shut up behind placarded doors.

Consider the praise songs we might compose
to antibiotics, immunization, the identification
and near eradication of microscopic organisms
that have blinded, maddened, paralyzed, and killed.

Yellow as zucchini flowers and, in their season,
as legion, school buses brake and collect,
brake and collect, at standard intervals
along the country's subdividing roads.

Late summer, the wind trending toward cool.
Early fall, the children heading back to school.

In the dream the doctors dreamed, no more
measles, mumps, rubella. Polio put aside.
Small pox persisting only in shelved vials.

Loaded up now, shocks dutifully enduring
the indignities pocked macadam delivers to a tire,
morning buses ferry our small gambles day to day.

In 1920, an American woman had less
than a 50% chance of seeing all her children
reach the age of 10. Late spring, the wind
trending toward warm. Early summer, already burning.

Lemons, tomatoes, peaches, zucchini: some crops
are like this. Tended correctly, what fruits
they produce, if they produce any, will seem,
to most of us, like overwhelming plenty.

Commute

He remembers the harp in his pocket and the tune
to a time-winding blues. Baby, I'm tied to you

forever. I'm tied to you forever. I can't quit you, baby.
I can't even put you down. This tunnel looks like love

gone hurtling into darkness. Across the track
a couple nods, appreciating something they can't

put their fingers on. He tucks the harp back in his pocket,
thinks to smile at her. It's all quiet for awhile but the wind

& then

their train.

oh my dear ones

in her sleep
in the passenger seat
at the wheel
slipped on ice
pulled under the pond
by the hands of a stranger
by the hands of a lover
by her own hands
her heart
due to complications
surrounded by family
after long illness
we don't yet know   why
we didn't know it would happen
this soon

Notes and Acknowledgments

"still in a state of uncreation" takes its title from a sentence in the "Anger and Tenderness" chapter of Adrienne Rich's *Of Woman Born: Motherhood as Experience and Institution*. The embryonic human in this poem is about seven weeks along.

"Cove Song" was commissioned by Kwame Dawes and Matthew Shenoda for the anthology project, *Bearden's Odyssey*. The poem is a response to Romaire Bearden's 1977 "The Sirens' Song," a collage of various papers with paint and graphite, from his series, *A Black Odyssey*.

"Ars Poetica after William Carlos Williams" is written in argumentative homage to one of my favorite demonstrations of the poet's desire for untethered freedom of expression: "Danse Russe."

"Mother daughter hour" borrows lines from *The Inevitable: Contemporary Writers Confront Death*, a book that includes work, quoted in my poem, by Wallace Stevens and J. M. Coetzee. The title of the book my daughter was reading that day must remain a mystery.

"Because it looked hotter that way" is shaped around the Gwendolyn Brooks poem, "We Real Cool." Thanks to Terrance Hayes and Peter Kahn for prompting and editing the anthology that includes this poem.

"Characteristics of Life" is written in conversation with "Author's Prayer" by Ilya Kaminsky and "Naturalist's Prayer" by Eva Saulitis. Eva is not with us any longer but, I am grateful, her books still are.

"One to Watch, And One to Pray" takes its title from one of the first rhymes I ever memorized. The poem, among my grandmother's favorites, enumerates the first four Gospels in their order: "Matthew, Mark, Luke and John, / the four posts my bed rests on. / One to watch, and one to pray, / and two to bear my soul away." Like most children's rhymes, this one both soothes and alarms.

"How Great the Gardens When They Thrive": When Dr. Danielle LaRaque was the President of the Academic Pediatric Association, an organization for which my father had recently served as President, she invited me to organize a poetry reading in honor of the association's 50th anniversary, which was celebrated at their annual meeting, held that year in Vancouver, BC. I was 36 weeks pregnant at the time I delivered the first public reading of this poem.

My gratitude to the editors and readers of the publications in which versions of these poems first appeared: *Academy of American Poets (Poets.org), Alaska Quarterly Review, American Poetry Review, Bearden's Odyssey, Because You Asked, Best American Poetry, Blackbird Literary Magazine, Boston Review, Caketrain, Callaloo, Connotation Press: An Online Artifact, Crazyhorse, D. C. Area Poets Against the War, Fifth Wednesday, Fourteen Guernica Hills, Iron Horse Literary Review, Kenyon Review, Kweli, New American Writing, Orion, Ploughshares, PMS (Poem-Memoir-Story), Poetry, Poetry Daily, Poetryfoundation.org, Spillway, The Golden Shovel, The Place That Inhabits Us, The Rumpus, Tin House, Verse Daily, Virginia Quarterly Review (VQR).*

Appreciation to: Colorado State University, The Diane Middlebrook Memorial Residency Fellowship of The Djerassi Resident Artists Program; The Hermitage Artists Retreat; the Jerome J. Shestack Award; San Francisco State University; the San Francisco State University Excellence in Professional Development Award; the Sustainable Arts Foundation Promise Award; U. S. State Department Speakers and Specialists Program.

I bestow abundant gratitude upon the human beings who have held my heart and shared this journey: my husband, Dr. Ray Black, and our beloved daughter, Callie; my parents, Drs. Claibourne and Madgetta Dungy; Lucy Anderton, Dan Bellm, Shane Book, Catherine Brady, Leslie Kirk Campbell, Lauri Conner, Lauren Crux, Tony Deaton, Rita Dove, Kathryn Dungy, Johanna Figge, Sean Hill, Brenda Hillman, James Hoch, Vanessa Holden, Leslie McGrath, Valerie Miner, Penelope Pellizon, Aimee Phan, Gregory Pardlo, D. A. Powell, Suzanne Roberts, Tammi Russell, Mary Ellen Sanger, Kristen Schmid, Mary Tesch Scobey, Samantha Shea, Erika Stevens, Suzanna Tamminen, Tess Taylor, Kimberly Wilson, Janet Yu, Maria Yusuf, all the Megans, and all of you.

Camille T. Dungy is the author of *Smith Blue*, winner of the 2010 Crab Orchard Open Book Prize, *Suck on the Marrow*, winner of the American Book Award, *What to Eat, What to Drink, What to Leave for Poison*, and a collection of personal essays, *Guidebook to Relative Strangers*. She is editor of *Black Nature: Four Centuries of African American Nature Poetry*, coeditor of *From the Fishouse: An anthology of Poems that Sing, Rhyme, Resound, Syncopate, Alliterate, and Just Plain Sound Great*, and assistant editor of *Gathering Ground: A Reader Celebrating Cave*. She is a Professor of English at Colorado State University.